Leaving Normal

New Women's Voices Series, No. 120

poems by

Gina Forberg

Finishing Line Press
Georgetown, Kentucky

Leaving Normal

New Women's Voices Series, No. 120

Copyright © 2016 by Gina Forberg
ISBN 978-1-944899-32-5 First Edition
All rights reserved under International and Pan-American Copyright Conventions. No part of this book may be reproduced in any manner whatsoever without written permission from the publisher, except in the case of brief quotations embodied in critical articles and reviews.

ACKNOWLEDGMENTS

Grateful acknowledgement is made to the editors of the journals and anthologies who first published the following poems. The poems, sometimes in earlier versions or with different titles, appeared as follows:

Anderbo Magazine, "My Son at Four"
Barefoot Review, "Bedtime Story"
Barefoot Review, "Swinging for the Fences"
Cancer Poetry Project 2 Anthology, "Picking Out Wigs"
Damselfly Press, "Smoking"
Inkwell Magazine, "Kid Problems"
Love You to Pieces: Creative Writers on Raising a Child with Special Needs, "Little Locomotive"
The Manhattanville Review: "My Son on the Tennis Court"
Mochila Review, "Blowing Glass"
Mochila Review, "One More Story"
Sage Hill Press, *All I Can Hold, a collection of poems on motherhood,* "Griffin"
Squaw Valley Review, "Starburst"

Editor: Christen Kincaid

Cover Art: Jackson J. Meryl

Author Photo: Jackson J. Meryl

Cover Design: Jackson J. Meryl

Printed in the USA on acid-free paper.
Order online: www.finishinglinepress.com
also available on amazon.com

Author inquiries and mail orders:
Finishing Line Press
P. O. Box 1626
Georgetown, Kentucky 40324
U. S. A.

Table of Contents

Blowing Glass 1

Jesus, Mary and Joseph 2

Smoking 3

Crow Call 5

Bedtime Story 6

Starburst 9

Kid Problems 11

Picking out Wigs 12

Little Locomotive 13

Swinging For the Fences 14

Morning Milk 15

My Son, at Four 16

Letter to Not Knowing 17

Griffin 18

Leaving Normal 19

One More Story 21

Slow Dance in the Kitchen 22

My Son Catching a Football in the End Zone 23

Shopping for Halloween 24

Mother's Engagement Ring 26

My Son on the Tennis Court 27

That Day 28

*FOR MY MOTHER ROSALYE
AND MY SON GRIFFIN*

….life's not a paragraph
And death i think is no parenthesis
                    -e.e. cummings

BLOWING GLASS

Two flights below
sand churns, rods rotate,
bubbles blow.

Molten and moving, we wait
for the belly of the bulb
to shape. Steel table, air pipe
etch lines around the neck.

Pontil breaks.

It can change in a second,
a goblet to a vase.

Dipped in water,
the body cools.

Another glass born,
so beautiful, so hard,
so easily broken.

JESUS, MARY AND JOSEPH

My mother spoke in clichés.
"A stitch in time saves nine."
"The squeaky hinge gets
the most oil."

Then there were the damnations.
"For Christ's sake." "Jesus, Mary
and Joseph." "For the love of God."

Married at twenty-one, pregnant
at twenty-two, thirty left her folding
laundry, ironing, cooking meals for five.
Jesus, Mary and Joseph carved themselves
into the grain of her wooden spoon.

She chased us around the kitchen,
her spoon flailing, her voice wailing,
"Jesus Christ get over here."

SMOKING

She smoked all the time.
She was after some wave of blue sea,
some ribbon of flowers,
some childhood afternoon
with the oven open, an orange October,
her own mother placing warm cookies
on a plate in the kitchen.

Outside the window crimson colors,
and suddenly she was out there
dancing in lightness,
a leaf, whirling, amazing.

She smoked all the time
through my grade school years:
some television show,
some voice in the background.

Once I stood in the doorway
watched her smoke a Marlboro
right down to her fingers.

My beautiful mother
caught in
a swirl
of smoke rings, my mother
a wheel of changing color
in a clouded kaleidoscope.

She invited me to take
a drag of her cigarette.
It was moist with lipstick.
On my small mouth.
Such breath.
A mountain climber exhaling
at 15,000 feet.
A hot air balloon lifting
from a cut cropped field
waiting, waiting for
the burner to ignite.

CROW CALL

They dive into the treetops
with their low pitched,
throaty squawks, drive off

the hawk, the owl,
build a nest of bark,
grass and twigs.

They snag treats
with long sticks, crack open
acorns with their bills.

They are teaching their young
how to be resourceful,
how to ward off predators
with their drawn-out caw.

I came to know the crow
as a child when
one summer morning
it poked its way
through the vinyl curtain
of my mother's shower.

When her cancer returned
five years later,
I thought of that bird

and how it cawed,
how it tried to warn us of a sleek,
black darkness to come.

BEDTIME STORY

When my mother knew
        it was her last night in her own bed
she had me put on the Egyptian cotton

sheets and dress her
        in her white silk pajamas.
I flattened the wrinkles

in the sleeves, held her arms firm
        and said, There, that should
soften the sores.

When my mother knew
        it was her last night in her own bed
she picked up her wedding photo,

smoothed her finger over my dad's face
        and said, He was so handsome, then patted
the empty space next to her and said, "Sit."

This was his side, and when
        I asked her if it was always that way,
she said, As long as I can remember.

And quite often those days
        she couldn't remember.
Struggling to retrieve words,

there was always a long pause
        followed by That, ...until she gave up,
pointed and shouted, That thing!

And I would deliver it to her
        like the most delicate orchid.
When my mother knew

it was her last night in her own bed
        she had me line up her medications
in alphabetical order on her night table,

looked at me and said, Can you believe
        all these pills? I never even took a vitamin,
licking her lips asking me to massage

her cracked mouth with ice chips
        and moist swabs. All those lipsticks
wasted, and when I asked her if she wanted

me to put some on her, she said,
        What for? Where am I going?
When my mother knew

it was her last night in her own bed
        she raised her hands in the air
as if conducting an orchestra.

I said, What? What is it?
        and she kicked the covers off
and rolled on her side, the bottom

of her pajamas soaked through.
        I cleaned her like I would clean
my two year old nephew, powdered

her privates
  and put her in a fresh nightgown.
Better, I asked, and she nodded.

When my mother knew
  it was her last night in her own bed
she pointed at her rosary beads

and prayer book.
  She asked me to read the prayer
to Saint Jude, patron saint of hopeless

causes, she, a woman of faith,
  rolling her fingers over the pearly white beads,
her bones digging into the down of the duvet.

When my mother knew
  it was her last night in her own bed,
she removed her hand from beneath

the covers and I held it, brushed her blue
  raised veins as we laid on our backs
like two lovers in a field of unstudied stars.

When her breathing became labored
  I was grateful
for the thunder of the subway, passing,

silencing her body. All night I lay there
  and when I heard
the rails rattle, I wanted one train

then another.

STARBURST

You were energy packed
inside me,
a speck of stardust
dizzy, tumbling, crashing,

but I could not keep you small.
My blazing belly baked you
and in seconds your time,
your universe began bursting
with wild, dazzling dreams,
dreams of Legos, fire trucks
and rubber ducks.

My milky way nursed you
and your mouth like a satellite
circled my nipples.

You, once a nebula
lost in space, a cloudy spot
on my womb
grew in size, in mass.
You were a supernova,
an unimaginable light
in a galaxy of stars,
but even light cannot
escape gravity.

We split, my eyes blind
to the dark matter,
the path pulling you
toward other bodies,
the girls, the drugs,
magnetic and spinning,
sparked and charged.

No one knows how one gets
sucked in. Sometimes black holes
are born when stars die.
Mother stars die every day.
It only takes an instant,
the right speed, a comet crashing
for the hungry young planet
to drink, to sip, to indulge
in the ecliptic sun.

KID PROBLEMS

Multiplication is easy for you at this young age.
Cells cemented to walls double, triple, permeate
plasma membrane. You have siphoned my spirit,
married my marrow, camped out in my womb.

Asking for my life back would be too much.

Eight months and counting. To what?
A cigarette? A beer? Xanax? Valium?
Outside you'll think it's all milk and nipples.
Let me tell you something: you're better off
where you are. In the baby business,
it's all about being on the inside.

Whatever you inherit, don't blame me.
If you're lucky, you'll get off easy
like Uncle Louie: bow legs, a stigmatism,
male pattern baldness.

Trust me. It's nothing a formula
or good smack on the ass won't cure.

PICKING OUT WIGS

She wanted human hair, nothing synthetic, length short to medium. Her head with its wisps and bald spots demanded a petite size after all those years of straightening her curls, using product for frizz control.

I flipped through the wigs in the Raquel Welch/Hair-U-Wear collection, "Courage," "Fortitude," "Hope," thinking these names alone might cure her.

The mannequin heads fascinated me: fiberglass regular, fiberglass long neck, fiberglass with arm, even a fiberglass Afro and all four with life like features—eyes, nose, mouth, hand-decorated eyelashes. The blank faced Styrofoam heads came free with the purchase of a wig.

After hours in the shop, the table covered with glossy print models, she chose one perm, one feathered, one eighties big. She added a rubber grip wire brush, a two-way pick, shampoo and conditioner.

Back home, I lined up the Styrofoam mannequins on her dresser, the backs of their naked heads reflected in the mirror, and gave each a name: "Dream." "Embrace." "Real."

LITTLE LOCOMOTIVE

We used to think of it as a game,
a chase, our own Olympic event.
Every morning at 6,
each evening at the hour of 6,
and all the time in between
my son ran circles around
our dining room table.
Ten laps became twenty, fifty,
one hundred. Griffin was intense,
intent on getting his morning,
afternoon, and evening exercise.
Sensory motor issues were the words
the occupational therapist used.
Our marathon runner, little locomotive
became subject to the habits of a dog.
Daily we groomed him, waited for
some bone-biting response. We bathed
him in lavender, chamomile, placed
pressure on his shoulders.
Today after we brushed him,
he rolled over, put a fist in his mouth,
spit it out, barked at the sight of our hands.

SWINGING FOR THE FENCES

My brother plays baseball to run from my mother's
cancer. He thinks each crack of the bat can resection
her liver, pitching no-hitters will reduce her white

cell count, and stealing bases will bring her home.
As she sucks on ice pops he practices his swing
in the batter's box, fields grounders on green diamonds,

kicks dirt in the dugout. I know she knows he will
never come into the room. I shake my head saying,
"It's not right," and she says, "No, he needs this."

I remember reading in "Gardening for Idiots,"
it is the acidity of the soil that determines the color
of the flower. A neutral PH creates cream, white.

In the garden hydrangeas bloom: pink,
blue, white, purple. "Some of them will
make it to Fall," my mother says.

Outside in the parking lot the halogen lamps hum
and the crickets insist on their summer song while
my brother waits in the car listening to the Mets' game.

MORNING MILK

He plucks the pacifier from between his lips,
arms reaching for the dancing dinosaur cup.
Fingers fanned, he spreads his hands around

humps, the thick of tails. Two-fisted, he tilts
the cup, mouths the spout like a cigarette, sucks
out the milk. His physical therapist says he should

be drinking from a straw by now, sipping
from an open cup. The drool should tell
her otherwise. The way he kisses open-mouthed

tells me. His speech therapist gives him tongue
exercises. He arches, rolls, shifts his tongue
from side to side. She has him blow whistles,

bubbles, kazoos. She pulls down his jaw, models
words like go and more. I offer him a warm
bottle. He lays his head between my breasts.

He sucks the fake nipple, formula dribbling
down his chin. They say dinosaurs cannot
nurse their young. They leave their eggs, save

energy for their own growth. Maybe I am
like the dinosaur. Maybe I keep the milk
for myself.

MY SON, AT FOUR

You could not sleep without it,
the whirl, recycled air.
It was a bedtime routine;
teeth brushed, story told,
lights out, fan on.

As a newborn, we left you
vibrating on the dryer, placed
you in a battery-operated swing,
drove you around the block
in your car seat as we acquainted
ourselves with the neighbors,
local road signs, varieties
of fauna.

At one, you swapped the dryer
for the tactility of buttons;
plastic, metal, wood. At two,
the lullaby song on the swing
stopped playing and by three
you invented your own road signs.

The fan has stayed with you.
The motor's belt is wearing thin.
Dust gathers in the vents.
We fear fire.

Outside the highway buzzes,
my husband's breathing becomes
inhuman. I cannot release my body
to sleep. The sheets rustle.

LETTER TO NOT KNOWING

I slip into my mother's bed, lay my head on the bumped up veins splitting her breasts. I tell her about the morphine, how it is an opiate, comes from poppy seeds, how it was used in ancient China for pain like natural herbs today, flaxseed oil, ginger, Echinacea. "No, no morphine," she says. "I want to be lucid to the end."

"What will happen when she starts to go?" I ask. "She will refuse food, solids then liquids. Her skin will grow cold and her organs will shut down." And I say, "What about her heart?" "It will weaken, the pulse will slow. If her breathing becomes heavy you might want to consider morphine."

GRIFFIN

The bible says you are an unclean bird. You mine
for gold in the flesh of my breasts, mouthing
milk, fighting off colds. You are of two natures.

Divine and human, you crawl around the kitchen floor,
grass stains on your knees, fingernails black
with earth. The bible says you are an unclean bird.

Body odor, pimples, clothes
on your bedroom floor, an excess
of papers crumpled behind

your steel locker door. You are
of two natures. Even though you cripple
flight, disgrace gait, you are pure gold.

If a man touches your treasure, you tear
him to pieces. The bible says you are a dirty bird.
But when you widen your wings,

you are a grown boy, my child,
a man, and when you leave my home
there will be nothing left of earth to hold.

LEAVING NORMAL

Tom Cruise was a functional illiterate.
He learned to read as an adult from L. Ron Hubbard,
Founder of The Church of Scientology.

Marilyn Monroe's breathy way of speaking was due to stuttering.
Jay Leno, a dyslexic, spoke French with a Scottish accent.
My son did not hear vowel sounds until he was two and a half.

John Irving was placed in the hands
of a psychologist for repeatedly failing courses
in language therapy while Yeats' father

flung a book at his head when he couldn't learn
to spell. My son's knuckles turned white
when he gripped his pencil, spelling "mother" "mudda."

Mark Twain confirmed, "I don't give a damn for a man
that can only spell a word one way." The American
Stuttering Foundation used Winston Churchill

as a pin-up boy for advertisements in medical journals.
Thomas Edison was thrown out of school for being dumb.
My son repeated kindergarten twice.

Jack Homer, the renegade paleontologist flunked
out of college seven times.
Albert Einstein couldn't speak until he was three.

Leonardo DaVinci wrote his notes backwards from right
to left in a mirror. The Beatles had their own syntactical lyrics.
"Wo ho, love me do." My son says "lub" when he means "love."

Branden Bremmet, boy genius, knew
the alphabet at 18 months, played piano
at three, graduated high school at ten.

When his parents returned home
from grocery shopping, they found him,
a self-inflicted gunshot wound to his head.

When my son says "fuck" instead of "truck," "weed"
instead of "read," I am grateful for the sounds he makes,
for the missed chords, for the imperfection of song.

ONE MORE STORY

No one thinks about the son, insomniac
at thirty, the middle-aged woman popping
Ambien or the thirteen-year old girl curled
at the foot of her parents' bed.

It begins with "one more story." Come week's
end, a mother lay sideways tossed and tangled
in sheets, her breast spooned into the curve
of her child's back. But last night, when

I put you to bed and you asked me to stay,
I didn't think about the thirteen-year old girl
who couldn't sleep in her room, who couldn't
go to sleepover parties.

I only thought about you, quivering,
how you clung to the buttons
on my shirt, curled your toes, and let them
swim in the bend of my knees.

SLOW DANCE IN THE KITCHEN

Clumsily he grabs my arm,
threads our fingers,
wraps his spare hand
around my baby fat waist.
Eyes a serious, recessive
blue inch up to my nose,
and he leads me, his arms
pointed, taut like a warrior
with a bow and arrow
toward the open window.
We spin in circles, feet light
on the cold tile floor
and I think of how I still
have to make him lunch,
drive him to the bus stop,
but when I look at his
eyelashes like butterflies
blinking, nothing is more
delicious than this moment
and when he dips me
and presses his lips
a little too long,
a little too hard
against mine,
I lose my balance,
grab his shoulders,
save myself from falling.

MY SON CATCHING A FOOTBALL IN THE ENDZONE

Dolphins with their sleek skin break from the surface of the sea. Some spray. I am buoyed by the beauty of their slapping tails.

The starfish grip me with their five arms. Even my feet, the white heat of surf and sand fuse.

Such delivery, such touch. It's a gift my clumsy hands, my lazy eye were not a part of him.

Every element in my body is charged. Each catch is a conversation, an echo returned, a channeling of life rising to the surface.

SHOPPING FOR HALLOWEEN

Walking down Fourth Avenue
in the East Village I catch
a glimpse of headless corpses,
nylon wigs, rubber masks
lining storefront windows.
Inside hang skeletons,
werewolves, and zombies.

When I was ten it wasn't
the trick or treaters,
blood-mouth vampires,
or lightning bolted Frankensteins
that scared my mother.
It was me, her little girl
dressed as GI Joe; camouflaged jeans,
belt loaded with plastic grenades,
doggy tag daggling
from my neck.

This year I'm marching in
The Village Halloween Parade.
I'm thinking Lindsay Lohan,
tanner, empty liquor bottles
around my ankles, baby powder
on my nose and a blow up
Samantha Rosen on my arm.

Perhaps, a Warrior Princess
with a brushed micro
suede mini dress
and embellished beads
or a Sexy Mexy
with rainbow haltered top,

breasts in a bundle
like the stork carrying
a baby to its mother,
my mother, a mother
who wanted me to marry,
have a husband,
give her grandchildren.

The stylist dressing
the mannequin suggests
something that's safe,
but makes a statement
like a half mask.

Perhaps, a festive Mardi Gras court jester
green, purple and gold tipped bells,
one who can manipulate language.

The fool speaks
in nonsenses,
misunderstandings
and puns
yet often tells the truth.

My mother thought being
gay was nonsense
and when I put on my masks
I became the fool, fool
for not telling her
otherwise.

MOTHER'S ENGAGEMENT RING

The bank manager opens
the steel gated door,
shows the locksmith
to the safety deposit box.
He marks it like a crime scene,
two chalk "X's," one on the keyhole,
one to the left of the box.
He lines up the drill bit.
Lock bracer breaks
and the door swings open.
And there it is: guilt
for wanting to sell it.
I slide the gunmetal box
through the cavernous walls,
carry it to a private room,
flip up the clip. More than I expected.
My husband's boating license,
my son's birth certificate,
my mother's charm bracelet
and the ring,
sitting in a slit of velvet
reset after my father died
into a swirl of fourteen karat gold.
I twirl it between my fingers,
think about my new life,
a relationship with a woman,
a child every other weekend,
the couch I would buy
for my new place,
and I think
maybe all we need
in life is a reset,
a reshuffling of the cards,
hope for a better hand.

MY SON ON THE TENNIS COURT

I am in love with his strokes, the hard right-angled
cross-court, the driving backhand down the line,

the drop shot that just clears the net, spins
backwards, gathers the crowd's applause.

Every serve is a deliverance of muscle and grunt,
a way of breathing, like the way his body rises

and falls in his sleep, in, out, a return to dream,
a rhythm in his racket, a sonata of strings.

I cannot fault him for loving something else.
High in the stands the summer sun slips

into the shoulders of the crowd, shade shifts
in shadows across the court. He tosses the ball,

arches his back, rockets his legs. Smack. An ace.
Right into the body. It's hard to return a ball

with no angle. Maybe that's why when he serves
it to me, it is perfectly placed, right in the sweet spot.

THAT DAY

A boy swung
on the worn threads
of the tire.

Above, a house
housed in bumpy
bent branches.

Sun sliced through
the wax paper
of July's lush leaves

and light loomed
across his supple
brown legs.

He could not
have been happier.

His mother's palms
moved hand over hand
across the black donut

spinning him
faster and faster
until the chains

formed a helix,
a strand of DNA
he and she shared.

Late that afternoon, the clouds
changed charcoal gray
and when they held hands

a lightness lifted
them. They could sky write
white their names

across the clouds.
He would ask his mother
to marry him.

The rain came.
She hurried him in,
wiped his wet head,

draped his little boy body
in a beach towel linking her limbs
with his on the couch.

Outside lightning flashed,
branches broke, logs laid
like a labyrinth across the tire.

When the storm ended,
the swing swayed in the shadows
of where their feet dangled.

Water pooled in the prints
below, puddles dark, dirty
slow to rise.

Additional Acknowledgements

Thank you to the following teachers, mentors, friends and organizations for your support and guidance in helping create these poems:

Lisa Bellamy, Rachel Nevins, Camille Rankine, Phillip Schultz, Sheila Welch, Carol Ann Davis, Juliet Latham, Michelle Cahill, Garrett DeTemple, Brittany DiGiacoma, Phyllis Shalant, Jim Forberg, Lisa Thomas, Pam Syndercombe, Karen Shugrue, Jenine Beck, The MFA Program for Writers at Manhattanville College, Squaw Valley Community of Writers, The Writers Studio and Finishing Line Press.

Gina Forberg recently received her MFA from Manhattanville College. She was a 2008 participant at The Squaw Valley Community of Writers and was short listed for The Margaret Reid Prize for Traditional Verse. Her 2010 fellowship with The Connecticut Writers' Project has led her to become a summer high school poetry workshop leader at Fairfield University.

She currently teaches at Saugatuck and Kings Highway Elementary Schools and lives with her family in Fairfield, Connecticut. This is her first book.

www.ingramcontent.com/pod-product-compliance
Lightning Source LLC
Chambersburg PA
CBHW060225050426
42446CB00013B/3169